Chad,

Merry Christmas to
you and your family
I hope you enjoy
this little book.
Thank you for being
a great Boss."
Cindy DeBruin

LET'S START OVER!

WRITTEN & ILLUSTRATED BY
CINDY DeBONIS

DEDICATED
WITH LOVE TO
MY SON,
GIOVANNI

THIS BOOK BELONGS TO:

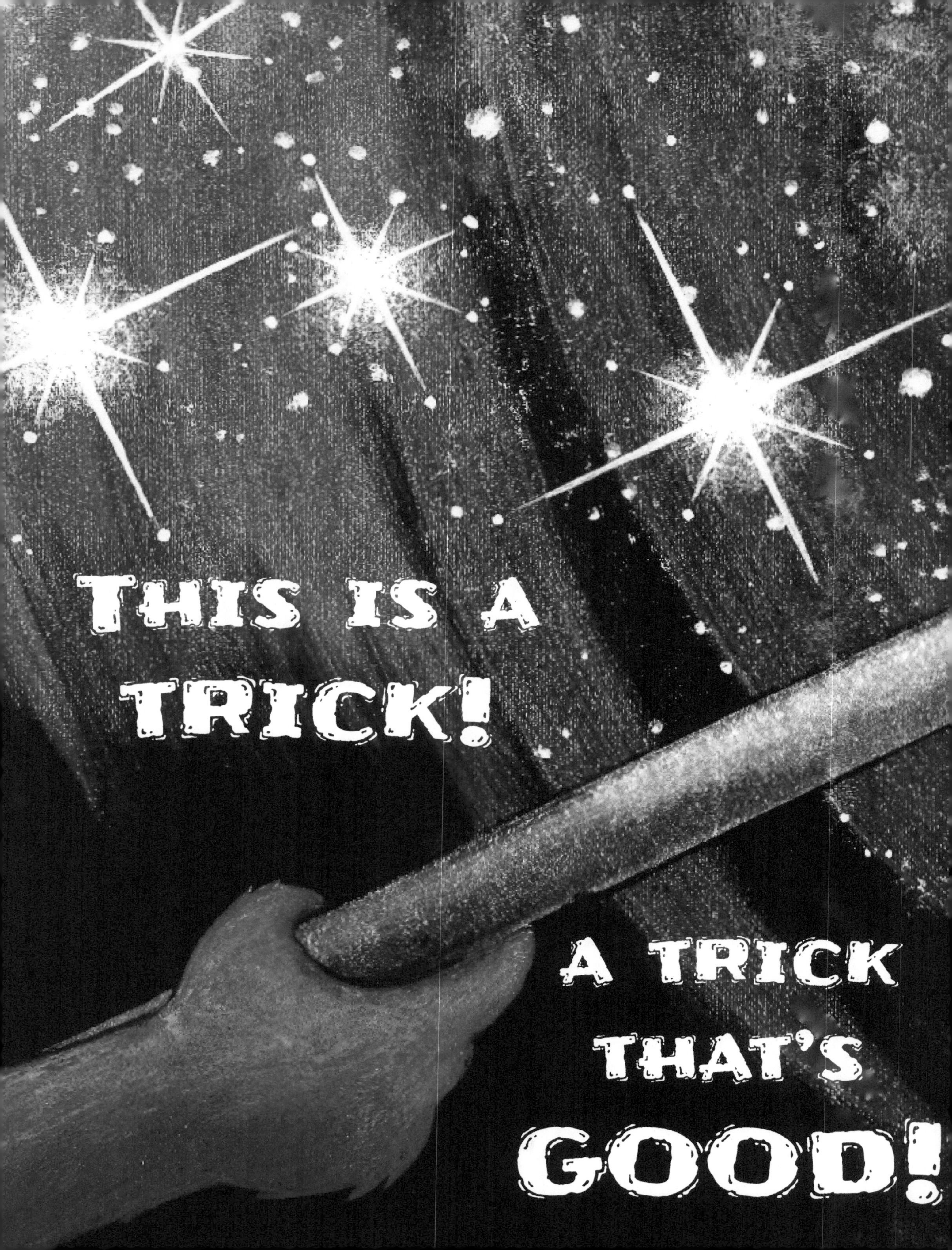

THIS IS A TRICK!

A TRICK THAT'S GOOD!

WHEN FAMILY OR FRIENDS GO HEAD TO HEAD

And DISAGREE with what the OTHER has said...

A TEAR IN YOUR EYE SHOWS SOMETHING IS WRONG... WHAT TO DO NOW???

IT'S TIME TO...

WAR GOES ON AND ON DEAR FRIEND... WE LIKELY FORGET WHY IT STARTED OR WHEN?

EACH SOUL MUST KNOW AND UNDERSTAND... THESE BATTLES WE FIGHT, SHOULD ALL JUST END!

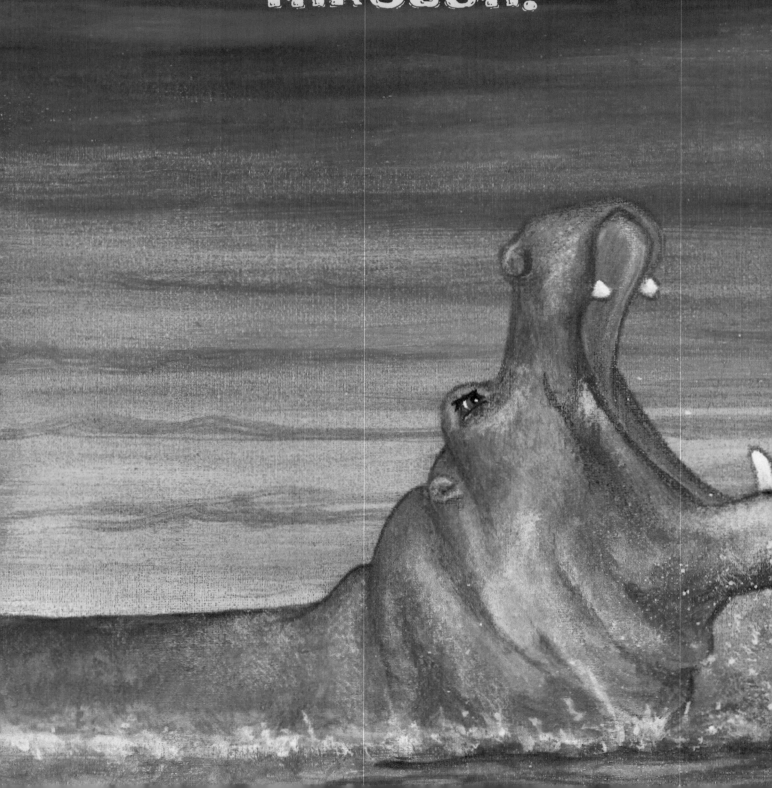

WHAT GOOD DOES IT DO
TO **FIGHT** YOUR WAY
THROUGH?

PERHAPS THIS TRICK
WILL WORK
WONDERS FOR
YOU!

LET'S STA

RT OVER!

IT'S EASY TO SAY...
ONE SIMPLE
SENTENCE CAN
MAKE A NEW
DAY!

IT'S OK to
DISAGREE!

IF WE WERE ALL THE SAME, A BORING PLANET IT WOULD BE...

CHANGE UP THAT MOOD, BE THE FIRST TO TRY... IT'S OK TO GIVE IN, IF LOVE'S THE REASON WHY

PERSONAL
OPINIONS ARE
HERE TO STAY, AND
FIGHTING
PROBABLY WILL
NEVER GO AWAY...

INDIVIDUAL THOUGHTS AND IDEAS MAKE THIS WORLD SPIN!
SO, "LET'S START OVER!" IS A TRICK THAT WILL WIN!

WIPE THAT
SLATE
CLEAN!
AND THEN
FACE THE FACTS...
LET'S
START OVER!
STOPS "ANGER"
IN ITS TRACKS!

ACKNOWLEDGMENTS:

Much thanks to my husband Ted and son Giovanni,
Kay-Jo and Edward Ramstead (Mom and Dad),
Kerri Walter (Cuzzy), Extended Family (Paddi and
Valentina Faubion),(Vickie and Tim Gardner) and
longtime dear friends in our Mt Baldy Village
community, who have consistently supported my
creative desires. Special thanks to Sara Klein for
her friendship and editing expertise, and Noah Witt
for his advanced knowledge in technology
and computer skills.

Text & illustrations copyright © 2021 Cindy DeBonis

Printed in the United States of America. First edition 2021.
ISBN # 978-0-5788755-9-0

CPSIA information can be obtained
at www.ICGtesting.com
Printed in the USA
BVHW020559260421
605847BV00001B/5